de:

THE DISCIPLE EXPERIMENT

6 SESSIONS
for helping students deepen their faith.

LEADER'S GUIDE

ZONDERVAN™

WWW.ZONDERVAN.COM

Youth Specialties

www.YouthSpecialties.com

The Disciple Experiment Leader's Guide
6 Sessions for Helping Students Deepen Their Faith
Copyright © 2003 YOUTH SPECIALTIES

YOUTH SPECIALTIES BOOKS, 300 S. Pierce St, El Cajon, CA 92020, are
published by ZONDERVAN, 5300 Patterson S.E, Grand Rapids, MI 49530

Library of Congress Cataloging-in-Publication Data

Yaconelli, Mike.
  The disciple experiment leader's guide : 6 sessions for helping
students deepen their faith / by Mike Yaconelli.
      p. cm.
  ISBN 0-310-25168-0 (pbk.)
  1. Church work with teenagers. 2. Christian teenagers--Religious
life. 3. Junior high school students--Religious life. 4. High school
students--Religious life. I. Title.
  BV4447 .Y315 2003
  268'.433--dc21

                                                    2002012275

Yaconelli, Mike, 1942-
The Disciple Experiment Leader's Guide: 6 Sessions for Helping Students
Deepen Their Faith/ Mike Yaconelli

ISBN 0-310-24488-9

Unless otherwise indicted, all Scripture quotations are taken from the *Holy
Bible: New International Version* (North American Edition). Copyright © 1973,
1978, 1984 by International Bible Society. Used by permission of
ZONDERVAN PUBLISHING HOUSE.

Web site addresses listed in this book were current at the time of publication.
Please contact Youth Specialties via e-mail *(YS@YouthSpecialties.com)* to report
URLs that are no longer operational and replacement URLs
if available.

Originally released as the *What Would Jesus Do? Leader's Guide*

Edited by Lorna Hartman and Dave Urbanski
Cover and interior design by Burnkit

Printed in the United States of America

01 02 03 04 05 06 07/ /10 9 8 7 6 5 4 3 2 1

CONTENTS

What you're holding is a six-session curriculum for helping teenagers understand what it means to really be a disciple in all the issues and decisions of their lives. It's nothing less than a spiritual challenge. Which is why the accompanying student journal is entitled *A Faith-in-Action Student Journal.*

The curriculum you're holding is designed to amplify or distill weekly the insights your students are getting from their daily readings in their journals.

Glance at the table of contents, and you'll see an opening and closing session (1 and 6), and four sessions in between. The idea is to kick off your students' 30-day spiritual experiment with session 1, conduct the middle four sections during your kids' 30-day challenge, then debrief them afterward with session 6.

At the top of each session is a "prep talk" of sorts intended for you. Then read through, instruct your Sunday school or small-group teachers to read through, the session complete, checking off (mentally or literally) the parts and options of the session you want to hit. There's probably not time to do everything listed in a session, so pick and choose what and your youth group are best at.

Talk about options galore. You'll find wild versions of calm activities (or calm versions of wild activities) . . . a few options that may take a hour or two before the meeting to prep for, but that add an unforgettable touch to the session . . . twists that make some activities more intriguing and others less complicated . . . alternative role plays and Bible studies designed to fit just about any youth group. And of course, as a youth worker you are well-practiced in adapting material to the needs and sensitivities of your own group—so by all means use that talent here, too, if you want to.

Each session has generally three or four reproducible pages of readings, discussion starters, etc. You have permission to photocopy all sheets for use in your own youth group. Here's to 30 days of faith-in-action that will bring your students (and you) closer to Jesus!

SESSION 01
THE ADVENTURE BEGINS

⩔

This lesson kicks off your students' 30-day adventure with Jesus through their Faith-in-Action journals. And there may be no better send-off than a vivid reminder that Jesus will likely be unpredictable during their experiment with him in the coming month. You can't put Jesus in a box, you can't cage him up, you can't anticipate his next move in your life with any certainty. Beneath it all, however, is love—expressed in words that have colored virtually all cultures, directly or indirectly, since they were first spoken by God to Israel, and later quoted by Jesus: *Love the Lord your God with all your heart and with all your soul and with all your mind...and love your neighbor as yourself.*

Matthew 22:35-40

One of them, an expert in the law, tested him with this question: "Teacher, which is the greatest commandment in the Law?"

Jesus replied: "Love the Lord your God with all your heart and with all your soul and with all your mind."

This is the first and greatest commandment. And the second is like it: "Love your neighbor as yourself." All the Law and the Prophets hang on these two commandments.

STEP BY STEP

Recruit three or four of your kids for some how-to demonstrations—changing a tire (with an actual jack and tire for visual effect), CPR or the Heimlich maneuver, a juggling demonstration, etc. Each demonstrator should explain the procedure step-by-step, keeping the explanation as simple as possible.

After the demonstrations…

Ask students to name other distinctive procedures. To get your kids thinking, toss out some of these ideas:

• What's the proper procedure for starting a car, according to the driver's ed. manual?

•• What steps do you take to get rid of a zit?

⁖ List the steps involved in making chocolate-chip cookies from scratch.

Then say something like this:

There are all kinds of step-by-step instructions for the little things in life. But when it comes to the really important things, it seems we get no help. *For example—*

• What's the proper procedure for dealing with a friend of the opposite sex who'd like to become more than a friend?

•• What steps should a person take to ease racial tensions at school?

⁖ What can you do to maintain a happy home life after your dad loses his job?

After a minute or two of discussion, explain that in the next 30 days your kids will be exploring a one-step procedure for dealing with life's most serious situations. And that one step is asking oneself, "What does it mean to be a disciple of Jesus?"

⩔

For maximum effectiveness, plan this activity with your recruits a day or two before the meeting.

⩔

NIGHT OF THE LIVING UNEXPECTATIONS

Since one of the major themes of this session is Jesus' unpredictable nature, why not turn the entire meeting into a string of unexpected events and activities? You can start with the relatively calm ideas listed here, and then go as crazy with this as you like.

UNEXPECTED SNACKS
Rather than cookies, chips, and pop, serve a nontraditional snack like breakfast cereal.

UNEXPECTED ATTIRE
If you usually dress casual for youth group meetings, show up in your best three-piece suit or the bridesmaid's dress you wore in a friend's wedding.

UNEXPECTED INTERRUPTIONS
A couple of times during the meeting, stop the proceedings cold and lead your kids in impromptu calisthenics sessions, aerobic workouts, or a jog around the church. Then resume the meeting as if nothing had happened.

UNEXPECTED GUESTS
Ask your pastor to drop in on the meeting for a minute, perhaps just to read the Matthew 22 passage (on this page, left margin). Ask an already graduated ex-youth group member to stop by with refreshments—and to lead one of the aerobics sessions.

EXPECT THE UNEXPECTED

Spend a few minutes talking about how the actions of Jesus, who walked the earth two thousand years ago, can make a difference in today's high-tech world, filled with complicated problems. Ask your kids to voice their stereotypes and preconceived notions about what Jesus was like and how he acted while he was on earth—always wore white, had long stringy hair, spoke kindly to everyone, etc.

After a few minutes, read the following excerpt from the Prep pages in the front of the Student Journal:

> **Jesus always did the unexpected.**
> **Jesus touched lepers when everyone else ran from them. He hung out with people he wasn't supposed to be around—traitors, children, prostitutes, and Samaritans. He didn't act religious—in fact, he made the religious leaders mad. He wasn't politically correct.**
> **He wasn't any kind of correct. The people around him said winning was everything. He said if you want to win, you have to lose. "Live as long as you can!" they shouted. He laughed and said, "If you want life, you have to die." Most every time Jesus spoke, the crowds responded with a resounding "Huh?"**

When you ask the question "What does it mean to be a disciple of Jesus?" think about the unexpectedness of his responses. Remember, Jesus doesn't think like everyone else thinks. Let your thinking run wild—just like his.

Hand out copies of **Tales of the Unexpected** (pages 10 -11), and ask kids to work in pairs to complete the quiz. After a few minutes, read through the answers as a group.

Now give your kids a chance to respond to some of these "Jesus realities," however new they may be to your students. If no one else mentions it, pose this question:

> **How can anybody today answer the question "What does it mean to be a disciple of Jesus?" when Jesus himself was so unpredictable?**

---

*Here are the answers to **Tales of the Unexpected**: 1.c; 2.a; 3.a; 4.b; 5.d; 6.d; 7.a; 8.b; 9.b; 10.a*

If yours is a smaller group whose members know each other well, this game's for you.

» I PREDICT

Before the session, hand out index cards and ask group members to write down five predictions of things they think will happen during the meeting. Tell them predictions must be fairly specific in order to be counted.

- *"I predict that we will pray during the meeting"—a vague, obvious, and therefore, no-good prediction.*
- *"I predict that Bob will begin his prayer with 'Our gracious heavenly Father'"—fairly specific, and therefore permissible.*

Other permissible predictions:

- *"I predict Karen will mention her cat at least once during the meeting."*
- *"I predict Russell will be the first one to the snack table at the end of the lesson."*

If a group member's prediction comes true during the session, he should call out, "Prediction!" (or "Fulfillment!" or "Ha! I'm a prophet after all!" or whatever exclamation suits your group). After you verify the prediction, that person is awarded a point. The person with the most points at the end of the lesson receives a prize.

This game provides a great opportunity for some good-natured ribbing, as well as for some backhanded affirmation. You can also contrast the predictability of your group members with the unpredictability of many of Jesus' reactions.

SESSION 01
THE ADVENTURE BEGINS

Before this lesson, make one copy of Questions on Matthew 22:35-40 (page 12)—and cut the questions apart into six slips.

ALL YOU NEED IS LOVE?

Have your kids quickly break up into groups of three or four. Give each group the same assignment:

> **In one sentence, sum up Jesus' philosophy—you know, his outlook on life.**

Obviously you're not looking for theological accuracy in these summaries—you're just trying to get a sense of how your kids view Jesus and his teachings. (Still, you may be surprised at the insight some adolescents are capable of.) After a few minutes have each group share what it came up with.

Then conclude by saying something like—

> **Did you know that Jesus himself was asked to summarize his teachings? His answer, in Matthew 22:35-40, is an excellent starting point for anyone who asks "What does it mean to be a disciple of Jesus?"**

Have someone read Matthew 22:34-38, then hand out question slips (see note at left) to each small group that your students formed earlier.

As the small groups share their answers, jot down comments (on blackboard, whiteboard, poster board, overhead projector, an unpainted wall) that particularly stand out to you—especially comments describing the imagined behavior of people who love the Lord or who love their neighbors. These comments will come in handy later as kids determine what Jesus would and wouldn't do in real-life situations.

PRACTICE, PRACTICE, PRACTICE

This week your students will begin their journaling about discipleship—and actually doing it. So now's a good time to give them a chance to practice deciding what he himself would and wouldn't do in real-life situations. Here are two scenarios for them to role-play. (Don't let the scripted gender keep you from using a male or female in any role.)

Ask for eight volunteers—each scenario will be performed twice, each time with a different pair of actors. For example, in "Tease You at the Pole" the first Karlene should respond in a way that Jesus definitely would not respond; the second Karlene should consider what Jesus would do in that situation, and react accordingly. Remind your volunteers to keep Matthew 22:35-40 in mind as they consider their Jesus-like responses.

Scenario 1.
TEASE YOU AT
THE POLE

❥

Karlene, a Christian, participated in
See You at the Pole each September
for the last three years. Her classmate, Jasmine, is not a Christian—
and delights in embarrassing Karlene
about all things religious. So immediately after this year's See You at the
Pole, in homeroom before class
began, Jasmine loudly asks Karlene
questions like, "Do you get a thrill
standing around holding hands with
other girls?" and "Did you pray for me
at the pole?"

Scenario 2.
NO THANKS

❥

Jorge is a Christian teenager who, every
week, does yard work free of charge for
the elderly Mr. Banson. Yet no matter
how hard Jorge works, it's never
enough—the old man always complains
that Jorge's work is sloppy and half-
hearted. Most of the time Jorge doesn't
mind Mr. Banson's ingratitude. Today,
though, Mr. Banson is being especially
critical and whiny—and Jorge just isn't
in the mood for it.

AS YOU WRAP UP THIS SESSION...

Offer kids a final word of encouragement as they begin their 30-day experiment. Remind them
that Matthew 22:35-40 ("Love God with all you have—and love your neighbor as you love yourself") is a good starting point as they try to answer the question "What does it mean to be a disciple of Jesus?"

Spend a few minutes figuring out what holds us back from a you-first attitude—and then
explore how we can give in (become disciples) to this attitude that Jesus exemplified during his
years on earth.

TALES OF THE UNEXPECTED

1. What did Jesus do when he heard that John the Baptist had been beheaded? (Matthew 14:1-13)

a. He restored John's head to his body and commanded John to come forth from the grave.
b. He called John's disciples to follow him.
c. He took off in a boat for some time by himself.
d. He comforted Elizabeth and Zechariah, John's parents.

2. What did Jesus say when the Canaanite woman asked him for help? (Matthew 15:21-28)

a. "I was sent only to the lost sheep of Israel."
b. "Follow me and you will have eternal life."
c. "Take courage! I have overcome the world."
d. "You do not know what you ask of me."

3. Why did Jesus curse a fig tree, causing it to wither? (Matthew 21:18-22)

a. He was hungry, and the tree didn't have any fruit for him to eat.
b. He knew it was the tree Judas Iscariot was going to use to hang himself after he betrayed Jesus.
c. He snagged his brand-new tunic on one of the tree's branches.
d. He was proving to the Pharisees that his power came from God.

4. On the night of his arrest, what did Jesus ask God to do? (Matthew 26:36-45)

a. Protect his disciples from the same fate he faced.
b. Come up with another way to provide salvation to the world—one that didn't require his death by crucifixion.
c. Bless all those who would follow him after his death.
d. Give him the strength to carry the cross to Golgotha.

5. During his trial before Pilate, how did Jesus respond to the false accusations of the chief priests? (Mark 15:1-5)

a. He carefully explained to the Roman officials and Jewish leaders that he was the Son of God, sent to provide salvation for humankind. He then backed up his claim by citing several Old Testament predictions of Messiah's coming.
b. He infuriated his accusers with his constant retort, "I know you are, but what am I?"
c. He answered questions with a simple yes or no.
d. He kept his mouth shut during the entire process.

6. What did Jesus say to the man who wanted to wait until after his father had died before following Jesus? (Luke 9:59-60)

a. He commended the young man for his tremendous faith.

b. He used the man as an example of how to honor one's father and mother.

c. He sadly informed the man that his father had just died that morning.

d. He told the guy to let someone else take care of the dead.

7. What did Jesus do when he entered the temple courts in Jerusalem just before Passover? (John 2:13-17)

a. He went ballistic, swinging at people with a whip and deliberately pushing over tables.

b. He tricked a money changer out of two denarii, which Peter then used to pay the taxes owed by the disciples.

c. He amazed the Pharisees by teaching from passages in Isaiah that only the wisest religious leaders understood.

d. He condemned the people who were still worshiping God in man-made temples.

8. What did Jesus do when the Pharisees brought him a woman who had been caught having an affair? (John 8:1-11)

a. He whipped a rock at the adulteress, missing her head by less than a cubit.

b. He started doodling in the dirt until everyone left.

c. He assured the Pharisees that the woman's sins would be judged in heaven.

d. He revealed to the crowd that the woman's chief accuser was the man with whom she had been having the affair.

9. When Jesus heard that his friend Lazarus was sick, he — (John 11:1-17)

a. healed Lazarus simply by saying to Lazarus' servants, "Your master has been made whole."

b. let Lazarus die without even trying to heal him.

c. called in sick for Lazarus at the temple where Lazarus worked.

d. corrected the messengers, pointing out that Lazarus' soul was sick, not his body.

10. What did Jesus do when he saw the mourners who were weeping for Lazarus? (John 11:17-37)

a. He got a little misty himself.

b. He said, "Let not your hearts be saddened. The man for whom you weep is not dead but merely sleeping."

c. He fed all 5,000 of them with just two fish and five loaves of bread.

d. He gathered them together at the foot of a large hill, where he then preached his famous Sermon on the Mount.

1. What's the difference between loving the Lord halfheartedly and loving him with all of your heart, soul, and mind?

2. Just what does it look like for one to love the Lord with all her heart, soul, and mind?
Describe her: How would she act? What would she do? What wouldn't she do?

3. How would a person who loves the Lord with all of his heart, soul, and mind be treated at your school? Why?

4. Imagine the most unlovable person you can think of.
Describe how to love that person as you love yourself.

5. Describe a person who loves his neighbor as himself.
How would he act?
What would he do?
What wouldn't he do?

6. How would a person who loves her neighbor as herself be treated at your school? Why?

SESSION 02
NOTHING TO FEAR?

⌄

There may still be innocence in childhood, but it seems to be getting rarer. And childhood seems to be getting briefer. There's no shortage of places to put the blame—the increased likelihood of a teenager's parents splitting up... economic trends which, for the first time in U.S. history, do not predict a higher standard of living for each successive generation ... a fearful view of a vicious world that much of the media seems determined to ingrain in us.

Yet this era is not the first to live under the cloud of dire fears. The God who sustained the Jews in captivity and the early Christians in persecution—the God who, because of his appearance in Christ, knows pain and therefore walks the painful path alongside us, whether that path is a totaled car, a totaled dream, or a totaled family— that God is somehow able to provide peace instead of fear, despite all the agonizing circumstances swirling around us.

⌄

Video interviews

Before this session, recruit a couple of trustworthy group members, put a vidcam in their hands, and send them out to a mall or other public gathering place to conduct some person-on-the-street interviews. The mission: to compile as many different responses as possible to this question: "What's the scariest thing that's ever happened to you?" Let the video team edit their own tape so that you play back only the cream of the crop for your group members during this session.

THE FRIGHTENERS

So what better way to begin a lesson about fear than by scaring your students? No, not by promising to liven up the next youth group party with your Barry Manilow tapes, but with a game. All you need is a chair, a blindfold, and a box full of creepy props—rubber snake, fake spider, small stuffed animal that can be easily mistaken for an actual mouse, etc.

THE RULES ARE SIMPLE...

A blindfolded volunteer sits in a chair in front of the group while a succession of contestants do their best to scare him (or at least make him jump). The contestants may use any (legitimate, tasteful) props they can find or any (legitimate, tasteful) strategy they can think of to make the kid jump. The only thing they may not do (beside using illegitimate or tasteless means) is physically touch the person in the chair.

The fun of this game comes from audience participation. Visually cue your group to emit startled gasps and nervous whispering—all intended to increase the volunteer's nervousness to the breaking point and increase the tension level as the victim waits to find out what's coming next.

⌄

NAME THAT FEAR!

Want an alternative to **Frighteners** for opening this lesson on fear?

All you need for the **Name That Fear!** game are several letter dice from the word game Boggle. The rules of this game are simple: a player rolls a letter die, then has five seconds to name something people are afraid of that begins with the letter showing on the die. If the player can't think of an acceptable response in five seconds, or if she names something that's already been mentioned, she's out. The roles of timekeeper (count "one thousand one, one thousand two...") and word judge can rest with you or the rest of the youth group. The game continues until only one player is left.

SHORT DIVISION

Need a quick, painless way to divide kids into small groups?

Try this. Since the main topic of this session is fear, have kids form groups based on which they're most afraid of—public speaking, heights, snakes, their parent showing up at school, whatever. (The first three are generally regarded as three of the most common fears people have.) If you can spare the time, you might even stage an impromptu, just-for-fun debate among the three groups about which fear is most rational.

EVERYBODY HAS 'EM

It's no secret that everyone has fears, some of them common, others very unique. Some fears are famous—like the daylight, crosses, and wooden stakes that Count Dracula fears.

Give your group members a chance to create their own Famous Fears lists. Divide the kids into small groups of three to five people each. Ask each group to choose a well-known person—real or fictional, dead or alive, local or national—and then come up with three fears that person would be likely to have. Each fear should be a clue to the person's identity. After a few minutes ask each group to read its list of fears as everyone else tries to guess who the person is.

Afterward say something like—

As you can see, only some of our fears are the sort that make us jump. Most of our fears are just everyday fears that are the result of circumstances beyond our control—situations that make us feel helpless.

Now to illustrate what you're talking about, with as much appropriate candor as you can muster, tell your group your three greatest personal fears. Generally, the more transparent you are in sharing your fears, the more honest your kids will be in a moment when they're asked to list their own fears. If you're a parent, you may fear your child not "turning out all right." If you're single, you may fear not getting married. Whatever your fears, do your best to explain how they make you feel.

We'll assume here that, thanks to your example, you've got your students at least somewhat comfortable with voicing their own fears. So now pass out an index card to each student, asking them to list their three greatest fears. No names (anonymity is important)—just fears. After a few minutes collect the cards, shuffle them, then read at random some of their fears. Encourage whatever discussion seems appropriate now and then, but under no circumstances allow anyone to mock or even make light of someone's fears.

DID JESUS FEAR ANYTHING?

Now, in reference to your students' readings the previous week in their Faith-in-Action Student Journals, ask them—

In which of the situations that you read about this week did Jesus feel some kind of fear?

Then ask—

Does it even make sense to talk about Jesus and fear in the same breath?

If you're not sure where to draw the line between the sorts of things you should confess and shouldn't confess to teenagers—what's appropriate honesty and inappropriate honesty—call someone more experienced in youth work than you are, someone whose opinion you trust, and ask them what they think.

You may want to give your kids a minute or two to look through their journals. In fact, if you think they'd be comfortable with the idea, ask a few of them to read their journal responses to one of their "What does it mean to be a disciple of Jesus?" questions. Use their responses to introduce the Bible study.

»

SESSION 02
NOTHING TO FEAR?

⌄

If your group members are hesitant to respond, read Luke 8:22 25, which describes a pretty scary situation. A life-threatening storm arises while Jesus and his disciples are out in a boat. So what does Jesus do? He uses his supernatural powers to calm the storm, making everything okay.

If no one else mentions it, point out that if Jesus had the power to calm a raging storm, it's likely that nothing really fazed him while he was on earth. So if that's the case, what good does it do to ask what Jesus would do in circumstances that were beyond his control when no circumstances were beyond his control?

⌄

*Snapshot of **Everyday Fears** (pages 18-20)*
- ***A Death in the Family.*** *Scared of death, scared of what to say to survivors, scared of the funeral.*
- ***The New Neighborhood.*** *Scared of starting at a new school—in a dangerous neighborhood.*
- ***The Moment of Decision.*** *Scared of where peer pressure is taking him, but too scared to just say no.*

⌄

Briefly explore—
1. *How the fear that results from focusing on our own survival usually spoils our Christian walk.*
2. *What it means to follow Jesus, who gave his life for us.*
3. *What it means for Christians to give their lives in standing up for something they believe in.*

But for a different perspective of Jesus' life on earth, ask two of your group members to read **John 11:1-16** and **Matthew 26:36-46** (page 17). Point out that in both of these situations Jesus faced real danger. In the John passage, Jesus risked his life to go back to Judea to help Lazarus. (The people of Judea had already tried to kill him once, and were likely to try again.) In the Matthew passage—Jesus' desperate prayer in Gethsemane, the night before he was killed—Jesus faced the prospect of the most agonizing suffering imaginable. And while Jesus obviously could have accessed the power to supernaturally overcome these situations, he chose to remain utterly human and forego using that power.

Which means he faced fearful situations just like we do.

Have your kids reassemble into the small groups they formed earlier. Instruct each group to put their heads and Bibles together for five minutes and—based on how Jesus dealt with his fear in John 11 and Matthew 26—suggest some ways for dealing with scary situations.

Later, as each small group shares its three-step plan with the entire group, try to create a master list (on a chalkboard or poster board) of the best ideas for kids to refer to during this lesson's next and closing activity. You may want to throw in your two cents' worth if the small groups don't mention these observations:

- **Pray about the situation. (Take a look at the serious praying Jesus did in Gethsemane.)**

- **Do what you have to do. (Jesus knew there were risks involved in going to Judea, but he went anyway.)**

- **Trust God to take care of you. (Jesus ended his prayer in Gethsemane with these words: "Yet not as I will, but as you will.")**

⌄⌄

DEALING WITH EVERYDAY FEARS

Once again have kids reassemble into the groups they formed earlier. Hand out the three scenarios in Everyday Fears (pages 18-20) to different small groups, then give them a few minutes to answer these questions (which are also on the sheets):

- What fears or insecurities are involved in this situation?

- What's the worst thing that could happen in this situation?

- What's the best thing that could happen?

- How might Jesus handle this situation?

After a few minutes ask each group to read its scenario and then share its responses. Encourage the rest of your kids to respond either positively or negatively to the small group's answers.

Wrap up this lesson by reminding kids that Jesus provided an excellent model for us to follow when we face frightening or uncomfortable situations. They can use some of the strategies they discovered during the meeting the next time they face a fearful situation—especially the "pray/do what you've gotta do/trust God" model mentioned above.

John 11:1-16

Now a man named Lazarus was sick. He was from Bethany, the village of Mary and her sister Martha. This Mary, whose brother Lazarus now lay sick, was the same one who poured perfume on the Lord and wiped his feet with her hair. So the sisters sent word to Jesus, "Lord, the one you love is sick."

When he heard this, Jesus said, "This sickness will not end in death. No, it is for God's glory so that God's Son may be glorified through it." Jesus loved Martha and her sister and Lazarus. Yet when he heard that Lazarus was sick, he stayed where he was two more days.

Then he said to his disciples, "Let us go back to Judea."

"But Rabbi," they said, "a short while ago the Jews tried to stone you, and yet you are going back there?"

Jesus answered, "Are there not twelve hours of daylight? A man who walks by day will not stumble, for he sees by this world's light. It is when he walks by night that he stumbles, for he has no light."

After he had said this, he went on to tell them, "Our friend Lazarus has fallen asleep; but I am going there to wake him up."

His disciples replied, "Lord, if he sleeps, he will get better." Jesus had been speaking of his death, but his disciples thought he meant natural sleep.

So then he told them plainly, "Lazarus is dead, and for your sake I am glad I was not there, so that you may believe. But let us go to him."

Then Thomas (called Didymus) said to the rest of the disciples, "Let us also go, that we may die with him."

Matthew 26:36-46

Then Jesus went with his disciples to a place called Gethsemane, and he said to them, "Sit here while I go over there and pray." He took Peter and the two sons of Zebedee along with him, and he began to be sorrowful and troubled. Then he said to them, "My soul is overwhelmed with sorrow to the point of death. Stay here and keep watch with me."

Going a little farther, he fell with his face to the ground and prayed, "My Father, if it is possible, may this cup be taken from me. Yet not as I will, but as you will."

Then he returned to his disciples and found them sleeping. "Could you men not keep watch with me for one hour?" he asked Peter. "Watch and pray so that you will not fall into temptation. The spirit is willing, but the body is weak."

He went away a second time and prayed, "My Father, if it is not possible for this cup to be taken away unless I drink it, may your will be done."

When he came back, he again found them sleeping, because their eyes were heavy. So he left them and went away once more and prayed the third time, saying the same thing.

Then he returned to the disciples and said to them, "Are you still sleeping and resting? Look, the hour is near, and the Son of Man is betrayed into the hands of sinners. Rise, let us go! Here comes my betrayer!"

EVERYDAY FEARS

A DEATH IN THE FAMILY

Five days ago, Sarah's little brother drowned while Sarah's family was on vacation in South Carolina. The family returned to their home in Ohio two days ago, but Marcie hasn't called or stopped by yet. That's kind of a problem, you see, because Marcie is Sarah's best friend.

Marcie feels terrible, but she doesn't know what to do. The truth is, she's scared—scared of seeing Sarah's parents and scared of saying the wrong thing to Sarah. Most of all, though, she's scared of going to the funeral and having to walk past the body. She's never been to a funeral before, and she's seriously considering not going to this one—even though it is for her best friend's brother.

> What fears or insecurities are involved in Marcie's situation?

> What's the worst thing that could happen in this situation?

> What's the best thing that could happen?

> How might Jesus respond if he were in Marcie's situation?

EVERYDAY FEARS

THE NEW NEIGHBORHOOD

Luis's mom got rooked in her divorce settlement with Luis's dad. His mom got custody of Luis; Luis's dad got everything else—the house, the cars, the savings account, everything. Despite the fact that his mom had no job and no source of income, the judge ordered Luis's dad to pay only the bare minimum for child support—an amount that wouldn't even cover monthly grocery bills. With no income and nowhere else to go, Luis and his mom moved in with Luis's grandparents on the west side of Chicago—in one of the most dangerous neighborhoods in the city.

Luis grew up in the suburbs, where he didn't have to worry about gangs and crime. The guys in his new neighborhood say Luis is too "soft" and is going to face some serious trouble in school. School starts in two weeks and Luis is scared—big time.

> **Name the fears or insecurities that Luis has.**

> **What's the worst thing that could happen in his situation?**

> **What's the best thing that could happen?**

> **How might Jesus respond if he were in Luis's situation?**

THE MOMENT OF DECISION

"C'mon, man, it's not like you're signing your name or anything," D-Man urged. "No one's ever gonna know who did it."

Chad paused for a moment, his finger resting on the nozzle of the spray can. He glanced around at N-Zain and Pos, who had already thrown their symbols on the freshly painted water tower. He then peeked nervously over the catwalk railing to the ground some 60 feet below.

Suddenly Chad wasn't so sure he wanted to spray-paint his new nickname, "C-Note," on the tower. The police were cracking down on graffiti vandalism. If word were to get out, Chad could face criminal charges. However, backing out of the mission at this point could be hazardous to Chad's health. N-Zain was known for his violent temper.

Pos noticed Chad's hesitation and quickly sprayed "C-Note" on the tower for him. "Now your name's up here whether you like it or not. You're one of us."

But that wasn't good enough for N-Zain. "You're not climbing down that ladder until you spray something," he warned Chad.

> **What fears or insecurities does Chad have in this situation?**

> **What's the worst thing that could happen to Chad?**

> **What's the best thing that could happen?**

> **How might Jesus respond if he were in Chad's situation?**

SESSION 03
TEMPTED

Like fear, temptation goes to the very root of our humanity—and especially of adolescent humanity. Parts of teenagers are waking up for the first time—hormones, for example, and abstract thinking, and the need to individuate. But the world gives adolescents no peace and quiet to get acquainted with these emerging aspects of themselves, no time to learn how deeply to trust these emerging "selves," before bombarding them with distractions, temptations, and seductions. It's like a 16-year-old getting into her car with a new driver's license and no solo experience—and then immediately trying to navigate her way from L.A.'s southbound 605 onto the San Diego Freeway. During the afternoon commute. On a Friday. In a stickshift when all she's ever driven is automatics.

And then there's temptation's dirty little secret. Of course, you never want your students to give in to temptation—but you know that when people do, their failure at the temptation game has the ironic ability of actually making them better persons, more compassionate and stronger Christians. It's one of those milestones of spirituality you don't exactly urge on your youth group, and for good reason. After all, isn't it your job to keep them from sin, not usher them into it for the sake of experiencing some good on the other side of it? But the good still sits there, waiting to be had.

Of course, there's more good to be had by not giving in to sin in the first place. And that's the message we all need to hear first.

A TEST OF WILLS

Start with a role-play activity. Recruit one Student and several Distracters. Tell the Student that in two days she has a final exam—which will count for half her total grade. So she needs all the study time she can get.

That's all for the Student. Don't tell her about the Distracters. Set her at a desk at the front of the room and ask her to pretend to study.

Now for the Distracters. Apart from the Student, explain to them that they are to get the person at the desk to blow off studying for the night. *Either let the Distracters think up their own ideas for how to tempt the Student, or give them some ideas to use:*

- **The youth group's Tom Cruise may try to seduce the Student away from her books by asking her out on a romantic date.**

- **A girl may talk about a one-day-only, 50-percent-off sale at Nordstrom (or Miller's Outpost, or another popular clothing store).**

- **Another Distracter may blatantly lie, telling the Student that the test has been postponed.**

- **Other group members may resort to bribery, threats, or blackmail.**

Whatever the method (short of physical harm), your group members' goal is to tempt the Student away from her books.

If, in the role play, the Student gives in to a Distracter, ask her to explain why that temptation got to her. If the Student refuses to budge, ask her to explain what temptations weren't tried that might have worked on her.

After the role play give your group members two minutes to come up with a list of 50 temptations. Have them shout them out while someone writes them down quickly on a whiteboard, overhead projector, etc. If they can list 50 legitimate and different temptations within, say, two or three minutes, give them a prize or extra snacks or something. Afterward, star the three or five temptations hardest to resist, and briefly discuss why they're the toughest.

TRAITOR JOES

Want a more active opener? Get your students' competitive juices flowing by pitting school against school, grade against grade, etc., in a good old relay race or similar contest. The twist that introduces the topic of temptation: pull aside three or four players before the game and make them a sweet deal if they'll discreetly throw the game. Start your bribes low and work up to whatever you can actually deliver. See how many players you can successfully tempt.

TEMPTING SCENARIOS

Now, in reference to your students' readings the previous week in their Faith-in-Action journals, ask them—

> **Which of the situations that you read about this week involved some kind of temptation?**

To find out how Jesus really did respond to a tempting situation, recruit three kids (narrator, Jesus, devil) to read Matthew 4:1-11 as it appears in **Did the Devil Make Him Do It? (page 25).**

Then say something like—

> **So what was Jesus' strategy for handling temptation?**

(Wait for responses, and briefly discuss if necessary. Be sure to end with this point:)
As you all noticed, Jesus immediately quoted his Father's Word back to Satan—and in so doing, never gave the temptations even a chance to settle in his brain. Because Jesus knew what was right, nothing could persuade him to do wrong.

You may want to give your kids a minute or two to look through their journals. In fact, if you think they'd be comfortable with the idea, ask a few of them to read their journal responses to one of their "What does it mean to be a disciple of Jesus?" questions. Use their responses to introduce the Bible study.

THE WORST PERSON FOR THE JOB

Let's play Worst Person. It's as easy as it's revealing. You call out a category—say, "Worst prom date." Now each person volunteers what, to them, the world's worst prom date would likely say. *Stuff like—*

- **I have to be home by 7:30 this evening.**
- **The guy at the rental place tried to talk me into a black tuxedo, but I said, "No way—if you don't have lime green, I'll find a store that does."**
- **You owe me $300 for this dress.**
- **I borrowed my sister's mountain bike so we can ride to the dance together.**

If your kids need to be primed with more examples, here are some other "Worst Person" categories and sample responses:

- **Worst superhero** (Do these tights make me look fat?)
- **Worst coach** (We just had these uniforms washed, so don't get them sweaty.)
- **Worst guidance counselor** (If your goal is to make a lot of money, you should consider youth ministry.)
- **Worst doctor** (Why don't you come back when you're not so sick?)

Save the last category—**Worst person to represent us before God**—
as a transition to the next part of the lesson . . .

If your youth group is too large for everyone to contribute their "worst person" responses, then bring up five or six different kids for each category and give this activity the feel of a panel or game show.

SESSION 03
TEMPTED

⌄

Hebrews 4:14-16

Therefore, since we have a great high priest who has gone through the heavens, Jesus the Son of God, let us hold firmly to the faith we profess. For we do not have a high priest who is unable to sympathize with our weaknesses, but we have one who has been tempted in every way, just as we are—yet was without sin. Let us then approach the throne of grace with confidence, so that we may receive mercy and find grace to help us in our time of need.

⌄

IF YOU CAN SWING IT
Candid Camera

Start this lesson on temptation with a few "Candid Camera" clips that you videotaped earlier. *What you need is—*

- Something tempting (fresh chocolate chip cookies, say, or Double Stuffed Oreos)

- An out-of-the-way place to set the cookie platter (an isolated corridor, an office or desk just off the main hall on Sunday morning.

- A place to conceal a vidcam on a tri-pod, aimed at the area of the cookie platter.

Tape a sign that says "for preschool snacks" (or something similar) near the cookie platter on a Sunday morning, load a 120-minute tape in the vidcam, turn it on, come back a couple hours later after services are finished and the church is empty—and see who you caught! With any luck, you just might have a revealing visual study in temptation (including all that goes with it—mixed emotions, cunning, guilt, deceit, resistance) for this lesson.

THE PERFECT COUNSELOR

Okay, now give them the final category, Worst person to represent us before God. But before you ask for responses, you may need to set the scene in heaven. God the judge in heaven, watching us here on earth. Satan the accuser, right there pointing out everything we do wrong and calling for God to punish us. Obviously, we need an attorney of some kind to represent us before God, giving him reasons why we should not be punished.

So now ask your kids to briefly describe the worst person for the job of our heavenly lawyer. You're not necessarily looking for humorous responses here, just honest answers. If your kids need some pump-priming, suggest ideas like these to get them thinking:

The world's worst heavenly lawyer—

- **Wouldn't care about the people he's representing.**

- **Would be afraid of or overmatched by his adversary Satan.**

- **Would have a bad reputation in the eyes of God.**

- **Would have no idea what he's talking about.**

After you get some responses from your kids, compare the qualities they mention with the high priest described in Hebrews 4:14-16 (see left). Remind them that in Judaism, a high priest is a kind of a lawyer in that he represents people before God.

Have one of your group members read the Hebrews passage. Then briefly discuss why Jesus is the best possible high priest we could have. Make sure that your students pick up at least these observations:

- **Jesus cared so much about us—the people he represents before God—that he gave his life for us.**

- **Jesus has already defeated Satan, his adversary before God.**

- **Jesus has a spotless reputation in God's eyes because— well, because he's God's Son.**

- **Because Jesus became human and lived on earth, he knows exactly what he's talking about when he defends us before God.**

HE'S BEEN THERE, DONE THAT

Divide students into three groups, then assign each group one of the following questions to answer:

GROUP 1

Why is it important for us to have a high priest who can sympathize with our weaknesses?

GROUP 2

What does it mean that Jesus was "tempted in every way, just as we are"?

GROUP 3

What was Jesus' strategy for dealing with temptation? *(You may need to refer this group back to Matthew 4:1-11.)*

After a few minutes have each group share what it came up with.

You might summarize the groups' responses by saying something like this:
Because Jesus, our high priest, faced the same kinds of temptation we face, he is prepared to give us help when we are tempted.

Now give your kids a chance to practice responding to temptation as Jesus would. When they gather into their small groups again, hand out copies of pages 26 - 28, assigning one of these scenarios to each group. Tell the groups to follow the instructions on the sheet as they prepare their role plays. Give groups a few minutes to figure out a rough direction to take from the scenarios they're given, then each group presents its role play. If there's time, give other groups a chance to respond.

DISCUSS

What are some of the positive results that can result from temptation?

What kinds of scars are left when you give in to temptation?

How might Jesus respond to someone who asks him, "What if I stumble?"

As you wrap up this session, remind kids that Jesus provided a model for us to follow when we face temptation. Encourage group members to use some of the strategies they role-played during the meeting the next time they face a tempting situation.

DID THE DEVIL MAKE HIM DO IT?

A reading of Matthew 4:1-11 for three readers (narrator, devil, Jesus)

NARRATOR: Then Jesus was led by the Spirit into the desert to be tempted by the devil. After fasting forty days and forty nights, he was hungry. The tempter came to him and said,

DEVIL: If you are the Son of God, tell these stones to become bread.

NARRATOR: Jesus answered,

JESUS: It is written: "Man does not live on bread alone, but on every word that comes from the mouth of God."

NARRATOR: Then the devil took him to the holy city and had him stand on the highest point of the temple.

DEVIL: If you are the Son of God, throw yourself down. For it is written: "He will command his angels concerning you, and they will lift you up in their hands, so that you will not strike your foot against a stone."

NARRATOR: Jesus answered him,

JESUS: It is also written: "Do not put the Lord your God to the test."

NARRATOR: Again, the devil took him to a very high mountain and showed him all the kingdoms of the world and their splendor.

DEVIL: All this I will give you, if you will bow down and worship me.

NARRATOR: Jesus said to him,

JESUS: Away from me, Satan! For it is written: "Worship the Lord your God, and serve him only."

NARRATOR: Then the devil left him, and angels came and attended him.

END.

✱

TO BE OR NOT TWO BEERS?

HERE'S THE SCENE...

Two freshmen have been invited to a juniors-and-seniors party. This is their big chance to earn some serious popularity points. All they have to do is get through the night without majorly embarrassing themselves. Both of the freshmen are Christians—but the person who invited them to the party doesn't know that. The host greets the freshmen at the door and holds out two plastic cups. "My cousin's on her way with another keg," she explains, "so we're trying to finish this one before he gets here. Go for it!"

HERE'S SOMETHING TO THINK ABOUT...

There are several different ways that this situation might be handled:

> THE FRESHMEN COULD WALK AROUND ALL NIGHT HOLDING THEIR CUPS WITHOUT ACTUALLY DRINKING THE BEER.

> THEY COULD REFUSE THE HOST'S OFFER BY CLAIMING TO BE RECOVERING ALCOHOLICS.

> THEY COULD DRINK SOME BEER—NOT A LOT, EITHER—JUST THAT ONE NIGHT, FOR THE SAKE OF POPULARITY.

> THEY COULD EXPLAIN TO THE HOST WHY THEY'RE NOT DRINKING.

> THEY COULD TURN DOWN THE DRINKS WITHOUT ANY EXPLANATION.

HERE'S WHAT TO DO...

Discuss the pros and cons of some of the different ideas for handling the situation. Then decide what Jesus would do in this situation and act it out for the rest of the group. Don't forget to portray how the rest of the partygoers might respond to the freshmen if they really acted as Jesus' disciples.

GAY BY ASSOCIATION

HERE'S THE SCENE...

A group of kids is sitting at a lunch table talking about Chris, a classmate. The hot rumor is that Chris is gay. Several people at the table offer evidence that they say proves Chris's homosexuality. Trey, however, isn't saying a word—and before long everyone else at the table starts getting suspicious. It seems that Trey (known around campus as a Christian) once invited Chris to church. Since then, the two have become casual friends. Just last week, in fact, Chris invited Trey over to spend the night, a fact no one at the table knows—yet.

HERE'S SOMETHING TO THINK ABOUT...

The dilemma for Trey is defending Chris's reputation without damaging his own reputation. If the Christian were to actually *defend* Chris...well, forget about it. (Don't even *think* about what might happen if someone were to find out that Chris invited Trey over for the night.)

HERE'S WHAT TO DO...

Discuss Trey's options. Ask yourselves, *"How would Jesus respond if he had a friend like Chris?"* Act out a scenario in which Trey reacts to the situation as a disciple of Jesus. Don't forget to show the positive and negative results of such an action.

A STERN REACTION

HERE'S THE SCENE...

Five guys are hanging around the locker room after basketball practice, just shooting the breeze. Maurice turns to Raymond and says, "What were those jokes we heard on the radio this morning?"

That morning Raymond had hopped a ride to school with Maurice—who, as usual, was listening to Howard Stern. Raymond listened to some of the things the shock-jock said, wondering how the guy could get away with such dirty jokes on the air. Maurice, of course, was laughing his head off.

Now Maurice can't remember the jokes and is asking Raymond, a Christian, to repeat them. Raymond would love to get the other guys laughing, but he's uncomfortable with telling the jokes.

HERE'S SOMETHING TO THINK ABOUT...

Strange as it may sound, Raymond doesn't have a lot of options here. If he says he can't remember the jokes, he'll be lying: He remembers every one of them. If he claims the jokes weren't that funny, the other guys will still want him to tell them. If he refuses to tell the jokes, the other guys will want to know why.

HERE'S WHAT TO DO...

Discuss the pros and cons of some of the different ideas for handling the situation. Then decide what Jesus would do in this situation and act it out for the rest of the group. Don't forget to portray how the rest of the partygoers might respond to the freshmen if they really acted as Jesus' disciples.

SESSION 04
ALL ABOUT ME

⌄

Schools lavish attention on scholars and jocks, churches laud the Jim Elliots and Mother Teresas and Billy Grahams, *Entertainment Tonight* and *People* magazine command that we kneel before the atheletes and supermodels as our cultural gods and goddesses.

No wonder most kids feel inadequate. Who can measure up to the Beautiful People, the Talented People? It's all most adolescents can do just to feel occasionally cool in the presence of the Faultless Few, be they on the Cineplex screens or across the aisle from them in algebra.

So it can be a hard nut to crack, trying to convince kids of their inherent worth to God. But once kids feel the Father's embrace, their self-image and identity take a turn for the healthy. This lesson can be a step toward making that happen.

⌄

*What you'll need for **Makeover**:*
- *Old sheet or blanket*
- *Table*
- *An array of makeup products— mascara, eyeliner, base, blush, lipstick, the works*

⌄

You may want to give your kids a minute or two to look through their journals. In fact, if they're comfortable with the idea, ask a few of them to read their journal responses to one of their "What does it mean to be a disciple of Jesus?" questions. Use their responses to introduce the Bible study.

BONZO PERSONAL DATA

Before this lesson prepare a list of off-the-wall, wacky, and obscure categories that deal with the identities, personalities, and tendencies of your group members. Now assign them an arbitrary point value. You may want to start your list with these:

Can roll tongue	03	points
Middle name begins with a vowel	10	points
Wearing shoes with laces	06	points
Born in an even-numbered month	05	points
Born in another country	11	points
Born on another continent	13	points
Been dumped by a boyfriend or girlfriend	15	points
Had name in the newspaper within the past year	12	points
Pierced body part	08	points

At the meeting, start by simply reading the first category. Anyone in the group who fits that category receives the designated number of points.

For example, you say —

BORN IN AN EVEN-NUMBERED MONTH—FIVE POINTS.

And any group member whose birthday falls in an even-numbered month then receives five points. The person with the most points at the end of the game is the winner.

Use this activity to lead into a discussion of the unique features that each person in the group possesses.

⌄

MAKEOVER

Everyone's seen this bit of silliness before, yet somehow it's always funny—and this time, topically appropriate too, since its point is how we allow others to mess up our self-image through thoughtless comments, peer pressure, etc. It's the old "Person Behind Your Back Whose Arms Become Your Arms While You Use Your Own Arms As Stubby Legs And Feet" camp skit. Staging can be as simple as draping a blanket or sheet over the "arms" person standing in back, or as polished as a hung sheet with two holes cut in it (for the arms of the person, standing behind the sheet, to stick his arms through).

Recruit two students (or, ahead of time, a pair of deacons or elders?) for Makeover.

Set the various makeup products on the table in front of the two recruits. The front person, whose face is showing, should announce to the group that she's going to demonstrate the proper way to apply makeup. Hilarity ensues as the person whose arms are sticking out of the sheet tries to blindly apply makeup to the other person's face. For full comic effect, the "face person" should give a running commentary on how to apply makeup.

NAME THAT HAND

Or Name That Elbow, or Name That Foot—an alternative to **Makeover** that's a bit easier to do and that can involve more people. Like **Makeover**, this guessing game demonstrates how we identify ourselves.

Decide whether it will be hands, elbows, or feet from which kids will guess their friends' identities. If it's hands or elbows, their owners stand or kneel behind a table, placing their hands or elbows on the table top, while a couple of students hang a blanket that shields the identities of the students behind the table.

For feet, participating students simply bare one foot, and place it forward, while the hanging blanket is lowered to hide them head to ankle.

THE ULTIMATE SELF-IMAGE

Now, in reference to your students' readings the previous week in their *Disciple Experiment Journal*, ask them—

> **Which of the several situations you read about last week involved some kind of self-image problem?**

Now ask them—

> **Do you suppose Jesus ever had any self-image problems? Why or why not?**

Encourage several kids to offer their opinions.

Ask someone to read Matthew 16:13-17 from a Bible. Use the following questions and comments to supplement your discussion of the passage.

> **1.** **What's going on in these verses? Was Jesus really worried about what other people thought of him? Why was he asking his disciples these questions?**

It's probably safe to say that Jesus was secure enough in his identity not to be swayed by other people's opinions. He was simply asking his disciples whether other people recognized the truth about him.

> **2.** **How would you describe Jesus' attitude toward himself and his identity?**

Granted, this is a weird question—but it just might draw out some provocative answers from your kids. Their responses may be helpful to them as they continue to ask themselves "What does it mean to be Jesus' disciple?" in various situations.

Here's one way to sum up Jesus' self-image: "I know who I am. If you don't know who I am, you're missing out on a lot." Run this idea by your kids to get their reaction.

Matthew 16:13-17
When Jesus came to the region of Caesarea Philippi, he asked his disciples, "Who do people say the Son of Man is?"

They replied, "Some say John the Baptist; others say Elijah; and still others, Jeremiah or one of the prophets."

"But what about you?" he asked. "Who do you say I am?"

Simon Peter answered, "You are the Christ, the Son of the living God."

Jesus replied, "Blessed are you, Simon son of Jonah, for this was not revealed to you by man, but by my Father in heaven."

SESSION 04
ALL ABOUT ME

⌄
A plan in the works

If you want more Bible study, sink your youth group's teeth into Jeremiah 29:11:

"For I know the plans I have for you," declares the Lord, "plans to prosper you and not to harm you, plans to give you hope and a future."

These words apply to Christians today— to your kids in the youth room—as well as to the nation of Israel. List and explore what plans God may have for his people today, and how having a God-given plan for one's life might affect a person's self-image.

⌄
Talking sense

If your group doesn't do well with serious role-playing, add a lighthearted spin to Identity Crisis! by replacing the character from the handout—like "Terri"—with an inanimate object. Use the youth group's mascot, or someone's favorite stuffed animal, or a caged pet. The conversation will be decidedly one-sided, and there will be more laughs—but if that's what it takes to prod your students into taking first steps in doing what Jesus did, this approach may be your ticket.

3. **How might having a clear sense of who you are help you when you face self-image problems?**

A person with a strong sense of identity is less likely to be influenced by the opinions of others.

4. **Describe people with strong self-images.**

Not necessarily cocky, but sure of their personal worth. They are confident that anyone who takes the time to get to know them would like them. They're also confident enough to ignore the negative comments of people who can't or won't look below their surface and see what they're really like inside.

5. **What would it take for you to cultivate a strong self-image?**
Ask your group members to answer this and the next question silently.

Not necessarily cocky, but sure of their personal worth. They are confident that anyone who takes the time to get to know them would like them. They're also confident enough to ignore the negative comments of people who can't or won't look below their surface and see what they're really like inside.

6. **How would your life be different if you had a stronger self-image?**

Give your group members some practice applying biblical principles to realistic self-image situations. Hand out copies of **Identity Crisis!** (page 33), then recruit volunteers who are to offer advice to the kids suffering from self-image problems in Identity Crisis!
You might say something like—

> I need someone to talk to my friend Terri here about a self-image problem she's having. If you'd like to know more about Terri's problem, read number seven on your sheet.

A volunteer from the group will then talk to "Terri" as a Christian friend, offering biblical advice and perhaps suggesting what Jesus would do in her situation. Encourage her to respond to the volunteer advice-giver as she imagines "Terri" would respond.

After each role play have the rest of the group offer some additional suggestions for what a Christian friend might say to the person suffering from an identity crisis.

If you have a small youth group...

BATTLE OF THE BANDS, ANTHEM OF THE NIGHT

Here's an alternative to Identity Crisis!—or an addition, if your group has the time and the interest. Have the kids bring a favorite song with them to the meeting. Divide the group in two any way you want—males and females, upperclassmen and underclassmen, casual dressers and fashion plates, school versus school, whatever.
Give each group a tape or CD player.

Now say—

Your mission, should you accept it (and you really should, you know), will be to campaign to make your song the official anthem of the meeting. Take 10 minutes to listen to your own song, then devise some reasons why your song should be made Anthem of the Night. Remember that tonight is all about identity, so your reasons and arguments should include an explanation of what the song says about self-image.

Teams can vote quickly on which song to champion. After the two groups have presented their cases to each other, an impartial judge (for example, a panel of your volunteers or adult helpers in attendance) decide which argument was most persuasive. Play the winning song—the meeting's anthem—at the end of the lesson.

As you wrap up this session, remind kids that Jesus provided an excellent model for us to follow when we face situations that affect our self-image. Encourage them to use some of the strategies they identified during this meeting the next time they face a self-image problem.

Quick – how might Jesus respond?

Here are some people with an identity crisis who need your advice about self-image from a caring Christian friend (that's you). How might Jesus repond? Well, it looks like it's you and not Jesus sitting here with your friend. So what would you tell them about what's important and what's not?

1. Jesse thinks girls will like him better if he buys himself a new Honda rather than keeps on driving the hand-me-down '83 station wagon he inherited when his parents bought a newer car.

2. Dan's older brother Kevin was Mr. Everything in school—homecoming king, three-sport letterman, you name it. Kevin graduated two years ago, and Dan's now a sophomore—but still, at least once a week, Dan is referred to as "Kevin Fulton's little brother."

3. Laticia has a learning disorder that's starting to affect her grades. There are classes at school that could help her with her problem, but Laticia refuses to go to them because she thinks they're for stupid kids.

4. Walter's not really a tough guy at heart, but he thinks he has to act like one at school to maintain the respect of gangbangers.

5. Anita's mom is a very heavy woman. During the school talent show, a couple of kids sitting next to Anita started pointing at her mom and laughing—not knowing it was Anita's mom. Anita is scared that at the next school function, someone will find out who her mom is.

6. Both of Lindsay's parents are alcoholics. Lindsay's not only ashamed of them, she's afraid she'll become like them.

7. Terri started smoking pot when she was 12. Last year she was expelled from school when they found weed in her locker. Since then, though, she's cleaned up her act and returned to school. The problem is, no one believes she's changed. Everybody calls her "Burnout."

8. The kids at school make fun of people who live in the town's mobile home park, calling them "white trash." Holly has never invited anyone to her house because she doesn't want her friends to know that she lives in a trailer.

9. Jeremy's father ran out on his family when Jeremy was six. Since then Jeremy's had a hard time believing anyone could love him.

10. Even though Carlos's brother uses a wheelchair, he's still able to go to school. But he needs Carlos's help to get from class to class. Perhaps because of that, Carlos doesn't have any close friends. Everyone just sees him as the nice kid who helps his crippled brother all the time.

SESSION 05
WHAT DOES IT MEAN TO LIVE A CHRISTIAN LIFE?

Say *evangelism* to a Christian, and there's no end of associations and images that the word conjures up. Evangelism is the Four Spiritual Laws…it's your pastor's weekly invitations to "come forward" at the end of Sunday services…it's visiting the homes of church visitors…it's bowing your head and praying silently before you dig into a restaurant meal…it's anything from a puppet show to a Christian rock concert that softens up the beachhead for a full-on frontal spiritual assault by the evening's speaker…etc., etc.

In addition to these proactive kinds of evangelism, the apostle Peter suggests a reactive one: *Always be prepared to give an answer to everyone who asks you to give the reason for the hope that you have.*

Which is to say, live your life, conduct your relationships and business as creatively, as honestly, as charitably, as righteously as you can. So when the questions come as to *why* you do this or that, you are prepared to explain how you try to keep God at the center of, if not the business itself, then at least of your motives and of yourself.

The point, of course, is don't keep quiet. Whether you initiate the conversation or reply to a question, let the cat out of the bag. Let people close to you know what fuels you, who loves you, who *you* love.

TRUTH OR DARE

Play Truth or Dare with your kids: one at a time, players are asked if they want a truth or a dare. If the player chooses truth, he must honestly answer a possibly embarrassing question about himself. If she chooses dare, she must perform a possibly embarrassing stunt.

With some carefully chosen questions and dares, you can have a lot of fun with this game. Here are some ideas to get you started on your own list of questions customized for your own group:

TELL US THE TRUTH!

- What's the most embarrassing thing you've ever worn to school—and what made you want to wear it?
- •• What's the most embarrassing thing you've ever had happen to you on a date?
- •‡ Tell us your most humiliating experience with food.
- ‡‡ Name a famous person that no one else finds attractive but you.

WE DARE YOU TO...

- Sing "I'm a Little Teapot"—with all the motions.
- •• Imitate a lizard for 60 seconds: crawl around on your belly while you make your eyes bug out and do the flickering reptile-tongue thing.
- •‡ Do a stand-up comedy routine for your group. Using only clean jokes, try to make us laugh. Oh, yeah—you have to shout each joke at the top of your lungs.
- ‡‡ Do an impression of Elvis Presley singing three verses of "Old McDonald Had a Farm."

*After a few rounds of the game, suggest that **Truth or Dare** is kind of like the Christian life: they both require people to answer unexpected questions.*

ALTERNATIVE ACTIVITY
Armless Charades

If you want an alternative to **Truth or Dare**, use Armless Charades to introduce the idea (developed later in this lesson) of communicating the Christian faith to others. Armless Charades is played just like it sounds: players are forbidden not only to speak, but to use their arms at all. From the shoulder down, no arm or hand action. As a result contestants usually flail about wildly as they try to communicate their assigned words or phrases. And if you can come up with the right phrases to be guessed, you'll have a pretty entertaining time.

The following lines, to be acted out by armless clue givers, are guaranteed to get your group laughing:

~ Your hair is on fire.
~ Your fly is open.
~ I think I'm going to be sick.
~ You've got something hanging from your nose.

Use this activity to introduce the idea of communicating our Christian faith to others.

THE REASON IS...

Ask one of your group members to read 1 Peter 3:15. Talk briefly about what kind of hope this verse means. Then ask two or three volunteers to relate to the group whatever questions people have asked them about their Christian faith. You may want to start them off with a couple personal anecdotes of your own.

Divide your kids into three groups, then hand out copies of the three **Got a Reason?** sheets (pages 38 - 40), assigning one of these scenarios to each group.
Instruct each group to answer this question:

> **How might your group's situation have turned out differently if the Christian had been prepared to give a reason for his or her faith—an answer to the people who questioned it?**

After a few minutes let each group share its response. Don't go into a lot of detail, because you'll be coming back to these **Got a Reason?** scenarios later in the session.
Now refer your group members to their Disciple Experiment journals. Ask them:

> **How many of the scenarios that you read about last week may have turned out differently if the Christians involved had been better prepared to give reasons for their faith—both to themselves and to the people who questioned it?**

THE BIG THREE

Explain that if we really want to know what Jesus would do in the **Got a Reason?** scenarios... or in the kids' journal scenarios, or in real life... we have to find out what Jesus said, especially about living a Christian life.
Here's one way to do just that: hand out index cards to your kids, then ask them to:

> **List what to you are the three most important aspects or responsibilities of the Christian life.**

Identifiers »

Here's a quick way to stimulate discussion about behaving in a clearly Christian way... or, in other words, to do what Jesus did. First ask your kids, *"How can you tell if a person is a Hoosier?"* or *"How can you tell if a person is a Raiders fan?"* Let kids shout out as many identifying characteristics of Indiana natives, both positive and negative, as they can think of. Shoot five or six such questions at the group: *"How can you tell if a person is a grandparent?"*, *"How can you tell if a person is a police officer?"*

Then the final question: *"How can you tell if someone is a Christian?"*

---

1 Peter 3:15

In your hearts set apart Christ as Lord. Always be prepared to give an answer to everyone who asks you to give the reason for the hope that you have. But do this with gentleness and respect.

You may want to give your kids a minute or two to look through their journals. In fact, if you think they'd be comfortable with the idea, ask a few of them to read their journal responses to one of their "What does it mean to be a disciple of Jesus?" questions. Use their responses to introduce the Bible study.

Pay attention to the characteristics your kids list for this category, for you can use them later in the session.

SESSION 05
WHAT DOES IT MEAN TO LIVE A CHRISTIAN LIFE?

ˇ

*The **Biggie** sheets, as you can see on pages 41 - 43, include the full Scripture passages as well as the questions. If you want your kids to look up and read the Scriptures from their own Bibles, simply mask the passages when you photocopy the sheets.*

After a minute or two, collect the cards and read the responses. Since you can expect the answers to at least include (in some form or another) prayer, Bible study, and love for others, organize the following Bible study around those three biggies.

Ask your kids to reassemble into the small groups they formed earlier. Hand out to each group one of the **Biggie** sheets (pages 41-43) with its assignment. Students should first read the Bible passages, then explore the questions. The questions are generally the same from each of these three sheets to the next. Here are the Bible references and questions:

Prayer
Matthew 6:5-15, Ephesians 6:18, Philippians 4:6-7

- What part does prayer play in the Christian life?
- •• Describe the example of praying that Jesus set for us to follow.
- •ᵉ How might prayer be useful to a Christian who's asked to give a reason for the hope she has or who's asked to defend her faith against people who are questioning it?

The Bible
Luke 8:4-15, Romans 15:4, 2 Timothy 3:16-17

- What part do reading the Bible and studying the Word of God play in the Christian life
- •• Describe Jesus' attitude toward Scripture.
- •ᵉ How might Bible study be useful to a Christian who's asked to give a reason for the hope he has or who's asked to defend his faith against people who are questioning it?

Loving each other
John 13:34-35, John 15:9-17

- How does loving one another fit into the Christian life?
- •• Describe the example of loving others that Jesus set for us.
- •ᵉ How might having a loving spirit toward others be useful to Christians who are asked to give a reason for the hope they have or who are asked to defend their faith against people who ar questioning it?

After a few minutes have each group share what it came up with. Encourage the rest of your group members to add their comments and ask questions about anything they don't understand or agree with.

ˇ

TIME TO SPARE?
Ad Agencies

If you have some extra time, add a creative element to the Bible study. Announce that each group is an advertising agency. One group has an assignment to promote prayer, another to promote Bible study, and a third group to promote loving one another.

The promotion may involve television commercials, radio spots, or print ads. The advertisements may use humor, drama, testimonials, or anything else your kids can come up with. The ultimate goal of the promotions is to encourage Christians to pray, study the Bible, and show love to another.

Give your group members some time to get their creative juices flowing. After several minutes have each group present and explain it's ad.

REASONABLE FAITH

While your kids are still in their small groups, ask them to look again at their **Got a Reason?** scenarios (pages 38 - 40). This time to create role plays that illustrate what Jesus would do in that situation. Remind students to include at least one or two of the Christian "biggies" that they just discussed… prayer, Bible study, love for others… into the proceedings.

After each group finishes its role play, talk about how being prepared with a reason… an answer… benefited the young person in each **Got a Reason?** scenario.

To close, pose the question:
(Students can either verbalize their responses, or simply consider your question quietly.)

> **What are three things you need, or need to do, in order to be better prepared when someone asks you for a reason for your hope, or questions your Christian faith?**

Encourage them to commit themselves to preparing for the inevitable questions and challenges to come.

ALAN »

When Alan accepted Christ at a church camp a few months ago, he became the only Christian in his family. Since that time, he's tried hard to show his family how much his life has changed. He refuses to watch movies or TV shows that have sex or swearing in them. He threw out all of his old CDs and now listens only to Christian music. He also started wearing T-shirts with Christian slogans on them.

Yet despite Alan's radical change of lifestyle, his parents never seemed to notice much of a difference in their son. Or if they did, they never said anything about it—until yesterday. Yesterday Alan told his parents that he couldn't go to a family reunion with them because people would be drinking there and drinking was against his beliefs.

Alan's parents were livid. "What kind of church tries to turn a boy against his own family?" Alan's dad asked.

Alan tried to explain what Jesus said in Luke 14:26 about disciples hating their fathers and mothers, but that just made things worse. Now Alan's mother is convinced that Alan is in a cult, and Alan's father accuses him of thinking he's too good for his family.

*

LI »

Li was the only one home when the Jehovah's Witnesses came to the door. When the men said they'd like to talk to Li about something "very important," she knew where they were headed. Yet she didn't want to be rude and slam the door in their faces, so she just said, "Uh… I'm a Christian. I go to Parkside Community Church."

"Well, that's nice," one of the men replied. "If you have just a few minutes, we'd like to show you some things in your Bible."

What should I do? Li wondered. *They're witnessing to me about their faith. Maybe I should witness to them about mine.*

"It will only take five minutes," the man repeated.

But what if they ask me a question I can't answer? Li thought. *Or what if I say the wrong thing and they jump all over it?*

"I'm not interested," Li blurted, and shut the door.

ANTHONY »

Pauly turned to face Anthony with a rock-hard expression.
"I don't want to hear anymore from you about church and God or
any of that stuff. You got it?"

"So what's the matter?" Anthony asked, trying to sound nonchalant.

"I thought you said you were going to pray for my grandma."

"I did pray for her. My whole church did."

"Then why did she die last night, huh?" Pauly asked, his eyes
welling with tears. "Tell me that."

"Aw, man—" Anthony began.

"I don't want your pity," Pauly interrupted. "I just want you to
admit that prayer doesn't work."

"But it does work," Anthony insisted.

"Oh yeah? When was the last time God answered one of your
prayers?"

The question took Anthony surprise. "Uh..."

"I thought so," Pauly said as he walked away. "Face it, man—if
God's up there, he ain't listenin' to us."

The BIGGIE of prayer

Matthew 6:5-15 • Ephesians 6:18 • Philippians 4:6-7

Read the Bible passages, then explore
these questions:

How does prayer fit into the Christian life?

**Describe the example of praying that Jesus set
for us to follow.**

**How might prayer be useful to Christians who are
asked to give a reason for the hope they have
or to defend their faith against people who are
questioning it?**

⩘

*And when you pray, do not be like the hypocrites, for they
love to pray standing in the synagogues and on the street
corners to be seen by men. I tell you the truth, they have
received their reward in full.*

*But when you pray, go into your room, close the door and
pray to your Father, who is unseen. Then your Father, who
sees what is done in secret, will reward you.*

*And when you pray, do not keep on babbling like pagans,
for they think they will be heard because of their many
words. Do not be like them, for your Father knows what you
need before you ask him.*

This, then, is how you should pray:

*Our Father in heaven, hallowed be your name, your
kingdom come, your will be done on earth as it is in heaven.
Give us today our daily bread. Forgive us our debts, as we
also have forgiven our debtors. And lead us not into
temptation, but deliver us from the evil one.*

*For if you forgive men when they sin against you, your
heavenly Father will also forgive you. But if you do not
forgive men their sins, your Father will not forgive your
sins.*—**Matthew 6:5-15**

*And pray in the Spirit on all occasions with all kinds
of prayers and requests. With this in mind, be alert and
always keep on praying for all the saints.*
—Ephesians 6:18

*Do not be anxious about anything, but in everything, by
prayer and petition, with thanksgiving, present your
requests to God. And the peace of God, which transcends
all understanding will guard your hearts and your minds in
Christ Jesus.*
—Philippians 4:6-7

The BIGGIE of the Bible

Luke 8:4-15 • Romans 15:4 • 2 Timothy 3:16-17

Read the Bible passages, then explore these questions:

How does reading the Bible, studying the Word of God, fit into the Christian life?

Describe Jesus' attitude toward Scripture.

How might Bible study be useful to a Christian who's asked to give a reason for the hope he has or who's asked to defend his faith against people who are questioning it?

While a large crowd was gathering and people were coming to Jesus from town after town, he told this parable:

"A farmer went out to sow his seed. As he was scattering the seed, some fell along the path; it was trampled on, and the birds of the air ate it up. Some fell on rock, and when it came up, the plants withered because they had no moisture. Other seed fell among thorns, which grew up with it and choked the plants. Still other seed fell on good soil. It came up and yielded a crop, a hundred times more than was sown."

When he said this, he called out, "He who has ears to hear, let him hear."

His disciples asked him what this parable meant. He said, "The knowledge of the secrets of the kingdom of God has been given to you, but to others I speak in parables, so that, 'though seeing, they may not see; though hearing, they may not understand.'

"This is the meaning of the parable: The seed is the word of God. Those along the path are the ones who hear, and then the devil comes and takes away the word from their hearts, so that they may not believe and be saved. Those on the rock are the ones who receive the word with joy when they hear it, but they have no root. They believe for a while, but in the time of testing they fall away. The seed that fell among thorns stands for those who hear, but as they go on their way they are choked by life's worries, riches and pleasures, and they do not mature.

*"But the seed on good soil stands for those with a noble and good heart, who hear the word, retain it, and by persevering produce a crop."—**Luke 8:4-15***

*For everything that was written in the past was written to teach us, so that through endurance and the encouragement of the Scriptures we might have hope.—**Romans 15:4***

*All Scripture is God-breathed and is useful for teaching, rebuking, correcting and training in righteousness, so that the man of God may be thoroughly equipped for every good work.—**2 Timothy 3:16-17***

The BIGGIE of loving each other

John 13:34-35 • John 15:9-17

Read the Bible passages, then explore these questions:

How does loving one another fit into the Christian life?

Describe the example of loving others that Jesus set for us.

How might having a loving spirit toward others be useful to Christians who are asked to give a reason for the hope they have or who are asked to defend their faith against people who are questioning it?

*A new command I give you: Love one another. As I have loved you, so you must love one another. By this all men will know that you are my disciples, if you love one another.—**John 13:34-35***

As the Father has loved me, so have I loved you. Now remain in my love. If you obey my commands, you will remain in my love, just as I have obeyed my Father's commands and remain in his love.

I have told you this so that my joy may be in you and that your joy may be complete.

My command is this: Love each other as I have loved you. Greater love has no one than this, that he lay down his life for his friends. You are my friends if you do what I command.

I no longer call you servants, because a servant does not know his master's business. Instead, I have called you friends, for everything that I learned from my Father I have made known to you.

*You did not choose me, but I chose you and appointed you to go and bear fruit—fruit that will last. Then the Father will give you whatever you ask in my name. This is my command: Love each other.—**John 15:9-17***

SESSION 06
THE ADVENTURE NEVER ENDS

⌄

Call this lesson Ebenezer. You know, the "Here I raise mine Ebenezer" from the hymn "Come, Thou Fount." The word harks back to the days of Samuel the prophet, on a day when the Lord routed the Philistines at Mizpah (1 Samuel 7:7-13), after which Samuel set up a stone and said, "Ebenezer!"—which is Hebrew for "Thus far has the Lord helped us!"

The rock called Ebenezer was a memorial, a memory aid. That rock reminded the Hebrews in that neck of the woods—or whatever Hebrews passed by en route to somewhere else—that God helped the Israeli army one day in that place. If God were to be silent for the next hundred years (which often he seemed to be), the people could always look to that rock and remember: Yes, we may not feel God's presence in this day, but feelings or not, he is God, and he is our God. Thus far has he helped us.

Make this final session an Ebenezer for your students. Stir kids to remember whatever transactions may have occurred between them and God, and then give them the opportunity to set the memory of those transactions in stone. They'll need the reminders of God's work in them during the critical years ahead.

TOTAL RECALL

The purpose of this final session is review. Your goal? To help your students remember what they learned during their 30-day adventure in The Disciple Experiment. So why not open the session with a memory game?

⌄

You may remember (no pun intended) playing this game yourself as a teenager. Settle your kids in a circle on the floor. To start the game, one person says, "I'm going on a trip and I'm taking a—," naming an object that begins with the letter her first name begins with.

For example, Jennifer says, "I'm going on a trip and I'm taking a jelly bean."

The person to Jennifer's left—let's call him David—continues the game by repeating what Jennifer said and adding an object of his own: "I'm going on a trip and I'm taking a jelly bean and a drainpipe."

And so on, around the circle. As the game progresses and more objects get added to the string, it becomes increasingly difficult for players to remember them all—although the alliterative link between the objects and the kids' names helps.

If a player forgets an object, he's out of the game. The person to his left then begins the next round by naming a new first object. Continue the game until only a few players remain.

IN THE REAL WORLD

Ask a few special guests to talk to your group members about carrying **The Disciple Experiment** into the adult workplace. Invite members of your church to offer personal testimony as to how they maintain Christ-like attitudes and make God-honoring decisions in their careers. If possible, try to put together a roster of guests from a variety of career fields—from doctors to sales reps, from lawyers to police officers.

No chance for live guests? Try videotape. Look for some recorded interviews with or testimonies from professional athletes or celebrities who are Christians. Ideally these interviews will include discussions of how these famous Christians are able to make decisions based on their discipleship to Jesus in fields known for greed and immorality.

POP QUIZ, HOTSHOTS

Now get some honest feedback from your kids about their 30-day experiment, particularly about how (if at all) it affected their thinking, their actions, and their relationships. *Keep your questions simple at first, asking things like—*

> **What's the most surprising thing you learned during your experiment?**
>
> **What have the last 30 days meant to you?**

As you progress, turn your questions into challenges:

> **Seriously, do you remember anything at all about what you read in the past month?**

Your goal here is to appeal to your students' pride and bravado—and to lure them into a pop quiz. "Just to test you and see if you really remember as much as you say you do." *When they agree to a pop quiz, point to one of the kids and ask,*

> **How might Jesus respond if he were threatened by gang members at school (or by skinheads, etc.)?**

After she responds, turn to the rest of the group and ask if they agree with her answer. If anyone disagrees, ask that person to offer a better answer.

If you get even halfway decent responses from your kids, continue the quiz for three or four more questions. *Here are more questions to ask:*

> **How might Jesus respond if his closest friends all started getting into sex, drugs, and partying?**
>
> **How might Jesus respond if someone at school spread the rumor that he was gay?**
>
> **How might Jesus respond if his dad got laid off and his mom wasn't able to work?**

Keep the tone of your questioning light and fun. Don't let kids feel embarrassed if they don't come up with the "right" answer. At the same time, however, keep your antennae out to see just how much your kids picked up from their 30-day experiment.

SESSION 06
THE ADVENTURE NEVER ENDS

⌄

A Disciple Experiment worship service—by students, for students
What better way to close this final session than with a worship service planned, staffed, and attended by no one else but you and your kids? Such a service will take some work—especially on the part of your group members—but the results will be worth it.

As an adult leader of the group, your responsibility in the service-planning stage should involve nothing more than delegating. Appoint one group of kids to take care of special music for the service. Assign another group the task of finding a speaker. Put yet another group in charge of announcements and Scripture reading. (If you really want to go all out with the service, you might even appoint another group to be in charge of communion at the end of the service.) The only thing your kids need to know as they plan the service is that all of the elements should somehow relate to the theme of "What does it mean to be a disciple of Jesus?"

If you've never experienced a student-led worship service before, you're in for a treat. Chances are you'll be surprised—and moved.

THE PURSUIT OF PERFECTION

Recruit two students to lead the Bible-study portion of this lesson, and give them each a copy of **Whatta Man! (page 47)**. One student can read both passages and the other facilitate the discussions, or one student can read Matthew 5:48 and facilitate that discussion, while the other student leads the discussion on the Philippians passage.

Offer yourself only for "consulting" if your student leaders get stuck with a tough question. Otherwise, let the kids run with the Bible study themselves.

⌄⌄

A PRACTICAL CONCLUSION

Get your students to pair off, then hand out copies of *Everyday People (page 48)*.
Assign each pair one of the people-situations on the sheet.

Explain that each pair of kids will perform two 30-second role plays. In the first role play, one plays the person on the sheet, while the other plays himself. This first role play should illustrate how the group member would respond to the person on the sheet if he didn't stop to ask himself what he should do as a disciple of Jesus in the situation. The second role play should illustrate a response based on what a disciple of Jesus would do.

After each pair has performed, ask the rest of your group members to comment on the scenarios, offering tips as to how the situation might have been handled even better.

As you wrap up this session—and the 30-day experiment—send your kids off with some form of special encouragement. Depending on what you want to do, this sendoff may involve something as complex as a special worship service designed especially for your group members *(see A Disciple Experiment Worship Service—by Students, for Students, at left)* **or something as simple and brief as a benediction prayer over your students, blessing them with the courage to do as Jesus would do during the coming year.**

Regardless of how you choose to end this session, make it clear to your kids that the adventure of asking *What does it mean to be a discple of Jesus?* **never ends.**

Mr. Perfect

Be perfect, therefore, as your heavenly Father is perfect.— *Matthew 5:48*

Okay, what do you think this really means — that Jesus (who spoke these words) actually expects us to be perfect like him and God? *Explain your answer.*

If you answered no to the first question, what do you think Jesus does expect from us?

What are the pros and cons of trying to imitate someone who's perfect?

Let's assume that, because God is perfect, Jesus is also perfect. So how does that influence the answer to our question "What would Jesus do?" in a particular situation?

Mr. Humble

Your attitude should be the same as that of Christ Jesus: Who, being in very nature God, did not consider equality with God something to be grasped, but made himself nothing, taking the very nature of a servant, being made in human likeness. And being found in appearance as a man, he humbled himself and became obedient to death — even death on a cross! — *Philippians 2:5–8*

Exactly what attitude of Christ does this writer encourage us to follow?

How did Jesus humble himself? How are we supposed to humble ourselves?

Describe how your life would change—your thinking, your attitude, your actions—if you truly humbled yourself like Jesus did.

From the *Disciple Experiment Leader's Guide* by Mike Yaconelli.
Permission to reproduce this page granted only for use in buyer's youth group.
Copyright © 2003 Youth Speciaties.

EVERYDAY PEOPLE

⌄

Here's a list of people you undoubtedly deal with, think about, or hear about during a normal day.

Your assignment is simple: How might Jesus respond to these people? Think hard—the answers you come up with may actually affect your life!

By the way, don't settle for vague answers (like "Uh, Jesus would show him love"). Think—really think—about your responses. Think of specific actions, concrete things to do for these people.

What would Jesus do for—

- **The weird kid in your class whom everyone ignores?**

- **Your friend who isn't a Christian—and plainly doesn't want to be?**

- **Your annoying brother or sister?**

- **The person you know who recently experienced a tragedy?**

- **Your worst enemy at school?**

- **Your next-door neighbor?**

- **The people in your town's or neighborhood's nursing home?**

- **The biggest troublemaker in your neighborhood?**

✱